The Empress Edit

Vogue meets Vice.
Dressed in clarity.
Stitched with edge.
Not soft.
Not subtle.
And definitely not
sorry.

CONTENTS

1. Greatest Hits: Emotional Houdini Edition
2. Gen X - The No-Bullshit Generation
3. A Reason, A Season, A Screenshot
4. Midlife, Solo, and Selectively Social
5. The Look of Love (and Loathing)
6. The Myth of the Chill Girl
7. Sex, Shame, and Serial Killers
8. The Ego Cleanse
9. The Death of the Hustle
10. Rage, Rejection, and Radical Self-Worth
11. The Power of Being Underestimated
12. Men, Money, and the Myth of Being Chosen
13. Age, Appearance, and Other People's Projections
14. Forgiveness, Forgetting, and the Final Block
15. The Empress Era

You don't wake up hating them. You wake up tired of pretending not to.

Love doesn't curdle overnight. It curdles in the little betrayals: the rolled eyes, a sigh, the dismissive shrug, the text they swore they didn't send. One minute you're trying to decode their ignoring you, the next you're googling "emotional manipulation" at 3 a.m. with mascara on your pillow and a knot in your chest.

You don't even argue anymore. Arguing implies effort. Now you just avoid.

And that's when you realise something terrifying: you're still in love with the version of them that existed in your head. The version they performed at the beginning. The one who held your hand in public and said all the right things. The one who doesn't exist anymore, if they ever did.

This isn't about heartbreak, it's about humiliation. About wondering if you imagined it all, or if they just got better at lying. You remember their smile, the glint in their eyes when they looked at you, the version of you that only existed in their orbit. And still, the disgust creeps in. Slowly, then all at once.

You thought it was love. It was performance art. And you were the whole damn stage.

So, this chapter? This is for the ones who stayed too long. Who settled for scraps. Who got called "irrational" for reacting to disrespect. This is where the rose petals rot and the crown slips back onto your head.

Chapter 1: Greatest Hits: Emotional Houdini Edition

"You're overreacting."
"You always twist things."
"I never said that."
"You're too sensitive."

Translation? You've made a point they can't defend, so now it's your fault for bringing it up.

They're not gaslighting you, they're editing the whole script and handing you the blame. This isn't a relationship; it's a psychological escape room where you keep finding yourself apologising just to restore peace.

You're not broken; you've just been professionally destabilised by someone who treats logic like a contact sport.

You start mentally recording conversations, second-guessing your own memory, and drafting texts in your Notes app like you're preparing for court.

By the time they call you a *psycho* (how original), you're fluent in self-doubt, but also gathering evidence like a woman on a mission.

And here's the thing: they don't need to be loud to cause chaos. A raised eyebrow, a delayed reply, a sigh, a passive-aggressive "K" can do more damage than a shouting match. It's death by 1,000 paper cuts, and you're the one bleeding out in your own bed.

When Obsession Turns to Ick

Remember when their name popping up on your phone made you smile? Now it makes you nauseous.

Love turns when the butterflies die and are replaced with dread. When you apologise for crying. When their "likes" feel like betrayals. When they tell you you're being "dramatic" while actively giving you reason to be.

It's not insecurity. It's a well-tuned gut instinct.

You start noticing things you once ignored: how they talk to people on the phone, how they downplay your success, how they suddenly dress better but treat you worse. You wonder if they're in love with someone else, or just themselves.

You spray the perfume, pull the covers off your head, and walk into the kitchen like it's the red carpet at the Met Gala, sipping a martini in last night's heels, glaring at the toaster like it owes you rent, hoping this will be the day they look at you the way they used to.

They don't.

They're on their phone. Probably texting someone who makes them feel interesting. Someone who didn't ask them to take the bin out. Someone they can perform for.

And suddenly, the quirks you once found cute make your skin crawl. The way they slurp their coffee, the way they breathe. The way they mispronounce "espresso." The way they refer to every ex as "crazy" (spoiler: you were always going to be next on that list).

You don't hate them yet. But the desire? Gone. Vanished. Like your patience and their last three apologies.

The Flashback Files

Mini scenes that hit like emotional jump scares:

They're texting someone else while sitting next to you.
That expressionless face when you cried.
The vacuum of silence after asking a vulnerable question.

They don't fade. They play on loop when you least expect it. Not memories, more like bruises that never fully heal.

Flashbacks don't ask permission. You'll be fine one minute, making your morning coffee, then suddenly you're reliving that night they walked past you in a club and didn't say hello. And you still went home with them.

You didn't just ignore the red flags; you stitched them into a quilt and called it intimacy.

Worse? You told your friends it was fine. That they were "just tired." That maybe you were being too much again. But your memory remembers. Every pause. Every side-eye. Every silent punishment for having feelings.

Flashbacks remind you that your standards weren't always this high. They remind you how low you had to crawl just to be tolerated.

The Mental Gymnastics Routine

"He didn't mean it like that."
"She's just a friend."
"It's just his sense of humour."

You become a full-time emotional contortionist, twisting yourself into ever-tighter knots so the relationship still makes sense on paper. But darling, you are not a Cirque du Soleil act.

You're a woman with receipts, instincts, and a group chat that's already voted him off the island.

You talk your therapist into believing it's "not that bad." You lie to your friends with a smile. You're not naive. You're just hopeful, and hope can be deadly when aimed at the wrong person.

You start bargaining. If I just stop asking so many questions, maybe they'll be nicer. If I give them space, maybe they'll miss me. If I stay quiet, maybe they'll realise I'm the one.

You're playing emotional Sudoku with half the numbers missing and blaming yourself for not solving it.

When Your Body Knows First

Your stomach clenches when they enter the room.
You flinch at their touch.
Your whole system tightens when you hear their voice. Or when the key turns in the front door.

The body always knows. Before your brain can admit it, your nervous system has already started packing its emotional bags. Your body doesn't lie. Unlike them.

You stop sleeping. Or you sleep too much. Your skin breaks out, your appetite changes, and your chest tightens for no reason. But it's not no reason. It's them.

And still, you wonder if you're imagining it.

Your friends call it intuition. Your therapist calls it trauma response. Your mum calls it "a woman's gut."

Call it whatever you want, it's your body waving the red flags long before your mouth dares to say the words: "I think this is hurting me."

The Walkaway

It doesn't happen all at once. It's not fireworks or screaming matches. It's small. Quiet. Practical. It's deleting the photos. Returning the hoodie. Unfollowing, not because you're petty, but because peace doesn't coexist with their presence.

You stop checking if they saw your story. You stop waiting for the apology you know won't come. You stop wondering what they think of you because frankly, you don't.

Closure is a unicorn. Peace is the real prize.

You don't need to win the breakup. You just need to exit the stage. No farewell tour. No teary playlist. Just a disappearing act so clean, David Copperfield would sue.

And when you do?

You don't just walk away, you strut, with lashes, lip gloss, and a look that says: "You were lucky I even noticed you."

And you do it all without theatrics. No dramatic goodbye text. No "I wish you well." Just the slow, steady reclaiming of yourself.

Your friends were right, by the way. You were batting way above your average. And now? You're retiring the whole team.

Because the biggest flex isn't moving on. It's not needing them to notice.

The Post-Breakup Delusion Phase

You tell yourself they'll regret it. That they'll come crawling back. That they'll realise you were the best thing to ever happen to their mediocre little life.

They won't. And even if they do, so what?

You rehearse what you'll say when they message. You imagine the apology. The tears. The public declaration. And then… nothing. Just nothing.

It's a slap in the face with a velvet glove.

You start seeing signs where there are none. Maybe that playlist was for me. Maybe that quote on their story was about us. Maybe they're just scared.

No, they're just gone.

But here's the power move: you move on without needing the last word. Because the last word doesn't come with peace. And your peace is worth more than their presence.

You don't need their regret. You need your freedom.

And one day, when you're laughing so hard your mascara runs and someone truly kind is looking at you like you're magic, you'll wonder why you ever thought that mediocre mess was worth your sparkle.

Because hate is still a connection. But detachment? Detachment is power.

You could walk past them in the street and not even flinch. You no longer need revenge, or an apology they'll never have the decency to give.

Because you finally realised:
You weren't hard to love. They were just unequipped.

Loving them was like upgrading a Nokia 3310 and expecting it to run iOS 17. It wasn't you. It was the hardware.

And darling, that is not your burden to carry.

Next chapter: Gen X - The No-Bullshit Generation.

Chapter 2: Gen X - The No-Bullshit Generation

We were raised on sarcasm, perms, and riding our bikes until the streetlights came on, and we still had better manners than most people today.

We are the mixtape kids. The landline loungers. Some of us, the latchkey legends who knew how to heat a frozen lasagna before we knew how to spell 'therapy.'

Born between burnout and Backstreet Boys, we were babysat by reruns and raised by people who told us to stop crying or they'd give us something to cry about. We don't need a mood board; we had a Year 9 folder covered in Smash Hits stickers and Tippex scribbles. We don't need a safe space, we had dial-up internet, dial tones, and disappointment served in a glittery pencil case. We are not like the others. And we're not trying to be.

No Gold Stars, No Guidance

There was no 'gentle parenting' back then. You got a pat on the back if you didn't set the house on fire, and a solid eyeroll or very stern call of your name if you dared speak up. Our childhoods were less "How does that make you feel?" and more "You'll live."

We learned resilience the old-fashioned way: rejection, red cordial, and being told to get over it.
Emotional support was a Fruit Box and a "you'll be right."

We didn't need trophies. Some of us needed therapy. But hey, at least we can laugh about it now and that's cheaper than a psychologist.

Independent, But Not Neglected

Now let's clear something up: not every Gen X kid was left to fend for themselves. Some of us had mums who were *there* every day, every detail, every scraped knee and every teen drama. The type of mum who didn't hover but handed you the tools to be independent. Who didn't sugar-coat life but gave advice so real your friends lined up at your kitchen table to get it.

Let's be honest, half your mates came over for her, not you. And fair enough. She told it straight, didn't play favourites, and made you think twice before acting like an idiot. That kind of mum raised warriors, empresses, not worriers.

Too Old for Cool, Too Young for Irrelevant

Now? We're in the middle. Between "Do I need Botox?" and "Is this perimenopause, menopause or post menopause?" Between raising kids and raising eyebrows at TikTok influencers named Bryxxlee.

We're the invisible demographic, until someone needs a stable friend, a sarcasm translator, or help resetting the Wi-Fi.

We don't want to be cool. We want to be left alone with our antibacterial wipes, a clean kitchen bench, and a decent Pinot.

Also, remember when being on the phone meant dragging a three-metre extension cord into your room and hoping no one picked up the other line? When your dad yelled "Get off the phone!" because you had been talking for hours, even though you had been together at school all day? We didn't FaceTime. We scheduled calls. And we respected our parents, not out of fear, but because they earned it.

No Time for Fakery

We have zero tolerance for BS. We smell it before it walks into the room. Maybe because we spent our formative years watching people pretend everything was fine when it so clearly wasn't.

Now we crave realness. Give us weird. Give us awkward. Give us honest. Just don't give us curated captions about self-love while secretly spiralling. We invented sarcasm. We see you.

And don't even get us started on people who "identify as a chair" for attention. We identify with being exhausted, underwhelmed, and *still more emotionally stable than you*, thank you very much.

The Rage & the Resting Face

We're tired. Not sleepy. Existentially tired. And also, slightly ragey.

Tired of pretending to care about things we don't. Tired of being polite when someone's being a moron. Tired of being told we should "embrace aging" while watching the world fetishise 22-year-olds with lip filler and zero credit history.

And the audacity. People giving unsolicited advice on things they've never lived through. People treating you like you're outdated because you don't speak emoji. People assuming we're out of touch when we've *seen more, done more, and survived more* than most of them can imagine.

We've been underestimated and overextended our entire lives. We're done. Not bitter. Just deeply, deliciously over it.

Stay in your lane.

Don't Mistake Silence for Approval

Just because we're not shouting doesn't mean we agree. We're just thinking. Judging. Filing your nonsense into the part of our brain labelled *"Oh, please."*

We used to argue. Now we sip our coffee and go, "Wow. Okay." That's not agreement. That's us choosing our peace over proving a point.

We've realised not everyone deserves our energy. Especially not people who chew loudly, post cryptic quotes, or wear sunglasses indoors.

Gen X, But Make It Empress

We don't want to go viral. We want to go to bed.

We don't chase trends. We chase authenticity, strong boundaries, and someone who knows how to send a text without 47 emojis.

We're also the friends who give advice you don't take. We listen. We advise. We warn. Then we watch you walk straight into chaos with open arms. Call us *The Friend Shrink* - but don't call us at midnight crying about a man we told you to block six weeks ago.

We've had enough of the chronic complainers. The ones who refuse to change but love to vent. Book a therapist, we're not your unpaid emotional concierge.

And yes, maybe we're a little hardened. A little blunt. A little too quick to cut someone off for saying "triggered" unironically. But we've earned that edge.

We grew up dancing to actual dance music. We wore cargo pants unironically. We dyed our hair with supermarket bleach and called it fashion. And through it all, we were *real*.

Real conversations. Real consequences. Real connection.

We're not here to perform. We're here to be real. And if that makes us intimidating?

Good.

Next chapter: A Reason, A Season, A Screenshot.

Chapter 3: A Reason, A Season, A Screenshot

Some friendships come with wisdom. Others come with a warning label and a four-hour phone call.

We used to think friendships were forever. Like a pinky swear with a glitter pen. But the older you get, the more you realise some friendships are just really well-dressed placeholders for trauma, ego boosts, or convenience.

There's the friend who only calls when their life is a mess. The one who disappears the moment yours is. The chronic canceller. The secret competitor. The friend who drains your battery but never asks how you are.

And still, you stay. Because history. Because you were there when she got her heart broken in Year 10. Because her mum died. Because you think loyalty means forever, not until it's one-sided.

Let's talk about it.

The Ghost and the Return of the Queen

You thought you were close. Until suddenly, you're not.

They stop replying. They stop engaging. But they're still watching. Still liking your posts, like you can't see behind it.

They ghost you, but not completely, just enough to keep you confused. It's friendship breadcrumbing. One minute you're soul sisters, the next you're an audience member in their highlight reel.

You want to ask what happened. But what's the point? If someone wants to disappear, they will, and if they cared, they wouldn't have.

When Loyalty Becomes a Liability

Loyalty is beautiful - until it turns into emotional servitude.

You show up. You go stay with them when they have a breakdown. You rearrange your life because they say they can't cope. You walk to the shop for them because they "can't move."

And then a man calls, and suddenly they've made a miraculous recovery and are out the door with a blow-dry and 6-inch heels.

You don't expect grand gestures. But a little something would be nice. A thank you. A return message. A fraction of the emotional care you've extended.

Instead, you're their support act. You're the pre-show. You're the friend who warms the emotional stage before the real distraction arrives.

Friends Who Don't Take Your Advice

You tell them what's coming. You lay it out like an oracle in a leopard-print robe. They nod, they agree, they say they will take action.

Then they do the opposite.

Cue the weekly sob story. Cue the drama recap. Cue the 11 p.m. messages about a problem you literally predicted three Tuesdays ago.

At some point, you stop advising. You start archiving.

Call me *Dear Diary* - because you're not listening, you're just offloading. And I'm too old to be your unpaid therapist with no results.

They can talk for four hours about their issues but will somehow lose signal when you bring up yours.

The Quiet Goodbye

Some friendships don't explode; they evaporate.

There's no blow-up. No final argument. Just slower replies. Shorter calls. Missed birthdays. A vague feeling that things aren't the same… and probably haven't been for a while.

You scroll back through your texts and realise you were the one holding it together. The check-ins, the plans, the listening ear, it was always you. And you're not angry. You're just done.

Letting go isn't petty. It's peaceful.

Making Peace with the Fade Out

Not all goodbyes are loud.
Sometimes they're just less texting. Less care. Less connection.
Until one day, you realise the thread is so thin it snaps.

It doesn't mean you're cruel. It means you're evolving. Your standards are evolving. And some people aren't meant to make the whole journey with you.

Some were a reason. Some were a season. And some were simply lessons with a time limit.

Next chapter: Midlife, Solo, and Selectively Social.

Chapter 4: Midlife, Solo, and Selectively Social

You're not lonely. You're finally left alone - and there's a difference.

Remember when being busy was a badge of honour? Back-to-back plans, brunches, birthdays, beach days, bottomless everything? Now? The idea of being double-booked makes your eye twitch.

Somewhere between 38 and 'Why am I still doing this,' we stopped craving noise and started craving peace. And not in a faux-spiritual Instagram way. Real peace. The kind that comes from not having to explain yourself, dress up, or be on.

You used to think a full calendar meant a full life. Now you see it for what it was - chaos accessorised.

The Great Social Filter

You stop showing up just because you're expected to. You cancel without guilt. You don't RSVP "maybe" - you RSVP "no" and then don't go. You don't fake energy for people who wouldn't notice your tranquillity. It's not antisocial. It's evolved.

You're not avoiding people. You're avoiding small talk, fake laughs, and splitting a bill with people who order lobster when you had a side salad.

And the group chat? Muted. For one year. Minimum.

You now categorise people into two groups:

Would I pick them up from the airport?
Would I lie and say I was out when they call?

If the answer is "ugh" to either, they're on probation.

You Choose Solitude Over Settling

You don't fear being alone, you fear wasting time with people who make you feel lonelier in company than a group chat full of people who 'forgot' your birthday.

You've done the whole 'go to the event and pretend it was fun' routine. The kind of night where you stand in the corner holding a drink, wondering if anyone would notice if you vanished mid canapé. Now? You leave the group dinner early and unapologetically. You say things like "I'm good for tonight" and "I'd rather not." Revolutionary.

You've stopped convincing yourself that being around people is better than being with yourself. Because you? You are excellent company.

The Shift from 'More' to 'Enough'

You no longer want to be the most liked person in the room. You just want to be the most *at peace*.

You've stopped saying yes out of guilt. You've stopped attending events out of habit. And you no longer feel bad for choosing your couch, your cat, and your Uber Eats pad Thai over being someone's emotional support extrovert.

Think solo carbonara over pity invites. Think carefully curated excuses for events that simply don't float your boat. Think smoulders that come with receipts, not retinol.

You don't need a crowd. You need clarity. And carbs.

When the Spotlight Turns Inward

Midlife doesn't mean fading out. It means finally seeing yourself clearly.

You stop performing. You stop shrinking. You stop wondering what people think of you and start wondering what *you* think of them.

You start asking better questions:

Do I even like these people?
Is this outfit for me or the algorithm?
Why am I still at this job?

The shine isn't about bronzer. It's about becoming allergic to anything or anyone that makes your soul itch.

You don't just reclaim your power. You repossess it with interest.

The Luxury of Saying No

No is a full sentence. No, I won't come. No, I'm not explaining. No, I'm not available for guilt tripping.

You no longer need permission to protect your peace. You stop apologising for cancelling. You stop cushioning the truth. You stop showing up out of obligation.

You say no. And it's delicious.

You say no to parties with bad lighting. No to plans made by people who always bail. No to "let's catch up" texts that are nothing more than calendar clutter.

You say no to anything that smells like emotional labour dressed as friendship.

Selective Energy Economics

Your energy is not a group voucher.

You budget your time like it's money. You don't hand it out to emotional freeloaders. You stop engaging in debates you don't care about. You unfriend, unfollow, and unsubscribe with elegance.

And it's not bitterness. Its boundaries.

You're not cold. You're cured.

You can adore someone and still mute their Facebook posts. You can wish someone well and still block them.

Midlife isn't the crisis. It's the clearance sale. And what's left is luxury.

Next chapter: The Look of Love (and Loathing).

Chapter 5: The Look of Love (and Loathing)

You wanted fireworks. You got silent treatment. You wanted partnership. You got PR management for someone's ego.

Love in your twenties was chaos wrapped in butterflies. Love now? It better come with emotional intelligence, a budget, and access to a washing machine.

You're not asking for much. Just someone who knows how to apologise without saying "I'm sorry you feel that way." Someone who doesn't leave you feeling like you're begging to be seen. Someone who texts back in full sentences and doesn't treat honesty like an allergic reaction.

Let's talk about love, lust, and why your standards are no longer negotiable.

That Couple Look

You know the one. That way he looks at her. That way, she lights up when he walks in. You see it in cafes, in movies, at weddings. And you think:

"Why not me?"

Then you remember the time you cried in front of someone, and they checked their phone. The time you tried to open up, and they made a joke. The time you wore that dress, and they didn't even look up.

You don't want perfection. You want presence.

You want the look that says: I see you. Not just when I need something. Always.

Romantic Rage

There's a rage that hits when you think about how little you accepted. How you once convinced yourself a breadcrumb was a bakery. How you read between texts, over-analysed tone, justified laziness as chill.

He wasn't reserved; he just didn't care. She wasn't mysterious, she was indifferent. You weren't too much. They were too underqualified.

You don't miss them. You miss the version of yourself that still had hope in them.

The Playlist You Deleted

Because every song felt like a personal attack. Because you made a playlist for someone who didn't even know your favourite colour or fragrance.

Because you danced alone in the kitchen, thinking about them, while they were out making someone else feel chosen.

You deleted it. But sometimes one of those songs sneaks in and you let it play - because you're not bitter. You're just remembering who you were when you loved with no return policy.

The Standards Reset

You've changed. You don't want someone who checks boxes. You want someone who sees through you and still chooses you every damn day.

You don't want a project. You want a partner.

You don't want to beg for consistency. You want it built in.

You don't want to wonder if they like you, you want to feel it, loudly.

If love doesn't bring peace, presence, and joy, *it's just decoration.*

The Turn-Off Parade

You used to give second chances. Now one cringe and it's curtains.

If he lifts his legs while you vacuum, it's over.

If she says "I'm just being honest" after saying something cruel, goodbye. If they don't do compliments, don't expect access.

Hot is great. But emotionally clueless with a six-pack is still a pass.

You don't care if they look like Brad Pitt and David Beckham's genetically blessed cousin, if they bring nothing but mess and ego, it's a no.

When You Become the One

You're not waiting to be chosen. You *are* the choice.

You don't need to be someone's everything. You just need to be your own enough.
You make your own playlists now.
You look at yourself like *you're it*.
You don't chase the look of love; you give it to yourself.

Because the look of love? It's in the mirror. And it's never looked better.

Next chapter: The Myth of the Chill Girl.

Chapter 6: The Myth of the Chill Girl

She doesn't exist. And if she does, she's heavily medicated.

We were told to be cool. To not ask too many questions. To go with the flow. To act like we didn't care, even when we were breaking inside. The 'chill girl' was the one who laughed at the jokes, didn't start fights, didn't have needs, just vibes and looked good.

She was a marketing campaign. A mirage. A mascot for male comfort.

Because God forbid a woman expects something.

The Lie We Lived

You were called intense for wanting clarity. Needy for needing reassurance. Crazy for reacting to disrespect.

All while he couldn't even commit to dinner plans.

You lowered your expectations to match his emotional availability. You made yourself small so he could feel big. You called it love. It was a performance, and you were the unpaid lead.

And let's be honest, he wasn't deep. He was just quiet. There's a difference.

You said things like "I'm fine" and "No big deal" while your soul was internally flipping a table.

You waited for him to 'come around'. He waited for you to give up.

You weren't chill. You were emotionally ghost-writing his comfort.

The Price of Pretending

Being chill came at a cost. You stayed quiet when things hurt. You laughed off the red flags. You played it cool so they wouldn't label you complicated.

You told your friends "it's fine" when it wasn't. You let things slide. You lost count of the times you said "no worries" when actually, you had *many* worries.

You didn't demand clarity. You didn't text twice. You didn't speak first. And you were praised for being "so easy-going," while internally you were doing backflips trying to seem unbothered.

You made plans around his schedule. You changed outfits because he didn't comment. You edited your personality to fit his preferences and then watched him go after women who didn't care about any of that.

But at least you weren't the girl who caused drama, right? Except you were. Internally. And silently. With migraines and insomnia, and the rage that builds from never speaking up.

You become a magician of self-abandonment. Disappearing parts of yourself just to be liked. Sawing your needs in half to seem manageable. Smiling through it all like it's your party trick.

Eventually, you realise: the only person you were trying not to scare off was the one you should've run from.

Cool Is Cancelled

Now? You don't want to be cool. You want to be *heard*.

You ask the question. You express the need. You say the thing that might make them uncomfortable. Because if your honesty scares them off, they were never going to stay anyway.

You're done doing emotional origami just to be palatable. You're not a doormat with high cheekbones.

You're not chill. You're *clear*. You're not low maintenance. You're *well-maintained*.

You're not afraid of the label 'too much' you're afraid of dying a slow death by self-suppression.

You're not here to impress, you're here to feel safe, valued, and sane.

You're not asking for a parade. Just respect. Just effort. Just basic emotional hygiene.

And if they call that high maintenance? Let them. You're not a DIY project.

The Rise of the Empress Energy

The new standard? Being real.

You're not mysterious, you're direct. You're not low maintenance, you're selective. You don't hold back to make others feel safe; you speak up so you can feel sane.

You're done dimming. Done diluting. Done nibbling on ego fragments and pretending it's a charcuterie board. You were always worth more. They just got used to the sale price.

But not anymore.

You're full rate now. No discounts. No Afterpay on your energy. No clearance bin for people who "don't believe in labels." The only thing marked down is your tolerance.

You've been cool. You've been chill. You've been silent. And none of it protected you from the wrong person.

So now? You're choosing fire over freeze. Boundaries over breadcrumbing. Power over politeness.

Because the chill girl doesn't get the crown. The Empress does.

She doesn't chase. She doesn't wait. She doesn't wonder what he meant by "lol."

She leaves when it's not right. She speaks when it matters. And she can be as pretentious as she likes and wears red lipstick to the grocery store, not for attention, but because she *can*.

She knows now that being respected is better than being liked. And being honest is better than being chill.

Because here's the truth: the chill girl dies inside for the comfort of others. The Empress lives loudly, even if it makes people squirm.

You've muted yourself long enough. It's your turn to raise the volume.

Next chapter: Sex, Shame, and Serial Killers.

Chapter 7: Sex, Shame, and Serial Killers

Because dating after 35 is equal parts disappointment and true crime risk assessment.

Let's talk about sex. And shame. And the modern horror that is attempting to connect with someone without being disappointed, ghosted, used, emotionally exploited - or found in a freezer.

You used to worry about what outfit to wear. Now you worry if this is the guy who will murder you. But hey, lipstick still goes on.

The Swipe Fatigue

You swipe. You match. You message. You talk. You plan. They vanish. Or worse - they don't vanish.
They turn up and talk about crypto and ex-girlfriends.

Every dating app conversation starts the same:

"Hey"
"Hi"
"How's your day?"
"You're Hot"
[insert existential scream]

You've run out of ways to feign interest in photos of motorbikes and selfies at the gym, flexing their muscles. You're not bitter. You're just exhausted. And aware that most of these men treat dating like scrolling ASOS: add to cart, forget it's there, never check out.

The Shame Spiral

You grew up in a time when sex was taboo and girls who liked it were labelled everything except normal.

Now you're supposed to be a sexual goddess who's simultaneously chill, empowered, nonclingy, hot, independent, and fun, but also demure, low mileage, and modest enough to meet someone's mother.

Too sexual? Slut.
Not sexual enough? Prude.
Have sex on date three? Desperate.
Wait until date ten? Playing games.

You literally cannot win. So, you stop trying to please the scoreboard.

The New Red Flags

He's 52 and has "just come out of something." Translation: He's emotionally constipated.
He's never had a long-term relationship. Translation: He doesn't know how to compromise and
thinks bed sheets wash themselves.

He "doesn't do labels." Translation: You will
cry in your car.

He sends unsolicited dick pics.
Translation: He's emotionally three and leading with his weakest character trait. (If I wanted to be underwhelmed, I'd check my tax return.)

Your standards aren't high. They're just *sane*.

You now look for:
Does he do the cleaning without being asked?
Does he have manners and not the "says sorry after yelling" kind?

Is he drowning in debt - like, owes money to people who don't have surnames? Does he talk about women like we're humans, not halftime commentary?

The bar is low, but at least it's no longer underground.

The Sex Itself

Sometimes it's great. Sometimes it's... motivational. As in,

"Motivational to never text them again." You used to fake it.

Now you fake *sleep* so they'll leave.

You know what you like. You're not shy. But you're also not performing. Sex isn't theatre. It's communication, chemistry, and ideally, eye contact and clean sheets.

You want sex that feels like connection, not just cardio.

The Murder Risk is Real

You tell your friends where you're going. You Google him. You park under a light. You text your best friend a code word just in case.

You laugh about it. But you mean it.

Because you're not paranoid. You're practical. You've seen the documentaries.

Modern dating is two people showing up and silently hoping the other one isn't emotionally unavailable - or a killer.

The Exit Strategy

You don't do long goodbyes. You do Uber bookings.

You don't send paragraphs. You mute, moisturise, and mind your business.

You don't explain why they didn't make the cut. You just trust your gut, pack your bag, and walk out with dignity (and possibly a piece of your self-esteem).

They can call it ghosting. You call it *self-preservation*.

The Power Move

You stopped looking for someone to complete you. You started looking for someone who doesn't deplete you.

And until then? You have your own bed, your own playlist, your own peace. You'll take orgasms - but only if they come with emotional literacy and a valid driver's licence.

You are not desperate. You are not difficult. You are not too much.

You are the full package - and you're no longer offering express shipping to the emotionally illiterate.

Next chapter: The Ego Cleanse.

Chapter 8: The Ego Cleanse

It's not a detox. It's a deletion.

Let's talk about ego. Not confidence. Not self-esteem. E-g-o. The part of you that gets defensive when ignored, offended when excluded, and deeply invested in proving a point to people who don't matter.

It's the voice that says, "Text him back just to show him you're over it." It's the part of you that wants to post a funny meme, so he sees it. The side of you that tells your friend, "No, I'm not mad," while you're absolutely furious.

We've all done it. But eventually, ego becomes clutter. And you start cleaning house.

The Performance Audit

You realise how much of your life has been a show. The outfit you wore to look 'unbothered.' The party you went to, so they'd hear about it. The laughs that were louder than necessary. The compliments you gave just to be liked.

You weren't living. You were editing.

You said yes when you meant maybe. You said maybe when you meant no. You curated your life like it was a brand campaign and called it "just being yourself."

You spent time with people who drained you just so you wouldn't be seen as antisocial. You smiled through backhanded compliments. You bit your tongue so many times it bruised.

The ego thrives in spectacle. But your peace lives in truth.

So now? You do less for show. You stop performing your happiness. You start protecting it.

The Likes Don't Like You Back

You posted it for the reaction. But when the likes came in, you still felt hollow.

Because likes aren't love. Comments do not care. That fire emoji isn't connection. It's noise. And you know the dance. Post. Refresh. Wait. Compare. Spiral.

We were taught to equate visibility with value. That attention was affirmation. But what good is being seen by thousands if none of them actually *see you*?

You used to chase validation like it came with a loyalty card. Now you can't be bothered to post.

You don't need to be seen by everyone. You need to be known by the right ones.

The End of the Revenge Era

You plotted your comeback. You fantasised about running into them looking incredible. You rehearsed your one-liner.

But then... You didn't care anymore. You didn't need them to see how well you were doing. Because you knew it. That was enough.

Revenge is exhausting. Being unbothered is lethal.

You used to think peace was boring. Now you crave it like a sold-out designer drop, only it actually fits.

And it's not that you're not capable of a savage takedown. You're just busy. You're booked and unbothered. You've got other things to think about, like your joy, your goals, and whether that one friend is truly supportive or just really good at pretending.

The New Power Move: Not Reacting

You see the bait. You don't bite.

You're not correcting the narrative. You're not defending your name in rooms full of whisperers. You're not proving you're fine, you're just being fine.

Not reacting doesn't mean you're weak. It means you're working on better things than your reputation.

You've stopped attending every argument you're invited to. You're no longer in the business of overexplaining your decisions to people who barely know the whole story.

You're allowed to walk away without an exit interview.

The Unfollow Festival

You mute. You unfollow. You archive. You block, not out of pettiness, but peace.

You don't need a curated feed of people who trigger you. You don't need reminders of who hurt you. You don't need to keep up with people you wouldn't text if your life depended on it.

Your social media isn't a museum of everyone you've ever met. It's a sanctuary. Treat it like one.

And you know what else? You don't owe anyone a heads-up. If they notice you're gone, maybe they'll finally notice what they were missing.

The Mirror Talk

You look in the mirror and see it: the weight you've been carrying isn't always heartbreak. Sometimes it's your own pride.

You've held grudges like they were heirlooms. You've stayed angry because it felt powerful. You've clung to stories where you were the victim, even when you'd long since moved on.

You've replayed conversations that ended years ago. You've drafted text messages you'll never send. You've imagined arguments that only existed in your head.

But ego doesn't heal. It performs.

You don't want to be right anymore. You want to be free.

The Empress Reset

An Empress doesn't argue with clowns. She doesn't justify. She doesn't prove.

She detoxes the ego the way she clears out her closet: no guilt, no second chances, just gone.

She leaves chats on read. She walks away mid-conversation. She lets people misunderstand her if it saves her peace.

Because you don't need to be liked, avenged, or validated.

You just need to be *free*.

You don't chase it. You write the final line and drop the pen. You don't hold onto people who need reminders of your worth. You don't negotiate with ego-driven chaos.

You let go.

You rise.

You clear the space and find – finally - there's room to breathe.

Next chapter: The Death of the Hustle.

Chapter 9: The Death of the Hustle

You can't self-care your way out of burnout when burnout is your baseline.

We used to glorify it. The 5 a.m. starts. The 12-hour days. The unpaid extra work and side hustles, and bragging rights disguised as mental breakdowns.

"I've just been so busy" used to be a flex. Now it's a red flag.

Because being exhausted is not a personality. And constantly pushing isn't proof of your worth.

Let's talk about the hustle. And why we're done with it.

The Hustle Hangover

You thought grinding was the goal. That if you just worked harder, longer, louder, you'd finally earn the right to rest.

Spoiler: the finish line kept moving.

You used to set an alarm to go to the gym before work, skip lunch, stay late, then log on again at 9 p.m. to "get ahead."

You weren't getting ahead. You were getting tired.

You didn't have a morning routine. You had a panic sprint. You didn't have ambition. You had anxiety with a Google calendar.

And for what? A standing ovation from people who'd replace you by Monday?

The Praise Addiction

You were so good at being "on" you forgot how to be okay.

You became addicted to the praise. The "you're amazing" messages. The boss calling you "a machine."

You were validated for your sacrifice. For your absence at birthdays. For answering emails during funerals. For staying in toxic environments because "they need you."

They didn't need you. They needed someone who wouldn't complain.

They called it dedication. It was dysfunction in a pencil skirt.

Rest is Not Laziness

You used to feel guilty for slowing down. For saying no. For taking up space that wasn't productive.

Now you know rest isn't weak. It's required.

You don't earn breaks. You're entitled to them.

You cancel things now. You protect your evenings. You close the laptop and don't reopen it just because someone said "urgent."

Sleep is strategy. Quiet is a boundary. Saying "I can't do that today" is not failure, it's a flex.

You Are Not a Brand

You don't need a personal brand. You need a personal life.

You don't need to be "marketable." You need to be well.

You don't need to monetise every passion. You don't need to build an empire. You can be enough without becoming a walking LinkedIn post.

Your hobbies don't need hashtags. Your Sunday afternoons don't need content. Your worth isn't tied to your output.

You're not a business. You're a person. And people need breaks.

The Identity Crisis

When you stop hustling, you realise how much of your identity was tied to output.

Who am I if I'm not constantly achieving?
Who am I if I'm not busy?
Who am I if I don't have five plates spinning at once?

You start to feel… weird. Lost. Like a balloon with no helium.

But then you breathe. And feel something softer rise up: stillness. Sanity. Sanity that doesn't require a to-do list.

You're not a machine. You're a masterpiece.

The Power of Enough

Enough money. Enough clients. Enough hours. Enough attention.

More isn't always better. Sometimes, more is just *more anxiety*.

You get to stop striving and start sustaining. You get to opt out of the rat race and into something softer, smarter, more honest.

You get to go slow. You get to do less. You get to not care what someone on the internet thinks of your productivity.

You don't hustle to prove your worth. You work in alignment with it.

The Empress Exit Plan

The new dream? Peace.

You're not chasing burnout. You're not building on broken boundaries. You're not glamorising struggle.

You're choosing joy. You're choosing stillness. You're choosing work that fits into *your* life - not the other way around.

You're setting boundaries with your calendar, your inbox, your energy. You're choosing clients who respect your time. You're choosing goals that feel aligned - not impressive.

You are no longer afraid of the quiet. You crave it.

Because the hustle is dead. And the Empress is alive, and finally, at rest.

You still work. But it's no longer about proving something. It's about building something real.

Something that doesn't cost your mental health. Something that leaves room for sleep, joy, and the occasional Thursday afternoon nap.

Because success with burnout is not success. It's survival. And you are done just surviving.

Next chapter: Rage, Rejection, and Radical Self-Worth.

Chapter 10: Rage, Rejection, and Radical Self-Worth

Because you're allowed to be angry. You're allowed to be hurt. And you're allowed to still like yourself anyway.

They tell us not to be mad. Not to take it personally. Not to "overreact."

But what if rage is the realest reaction you have? What if rejection hurts because you *cared*? What if your self-worth doesn't mean floating above pain, it means walking through it with your crown intact?

Let's talk about rage, rejection, and the new era of self-worth that doesn't need approval, applause, or permission.

Rage Is Not a Problem to Fix

You've spent years bottling it. Diluting it. Smiling through it. "It's fine," you'd say, while quietly suppressing an emotional riot.

But rage isn't something to be ashamed of. It's information. It's your body saying, "This is not okay."

You're not too angry. You're finally just not numb.

You're not unstable. You're *awake*.

Your rage is sacred. Let it speak.

Because beneath the fury is usually grief. And beneath the grief is usually love. Rage isn't the absence of emotional intelligence; it's proof of it.

You cared. That's why it burns.

The Slow Burn of Rejection

It's not just heartbreak. It's humiliation. It's "What did I miss?"

It's checking your phone more than you should. It's the emotional hangover in three dots and no reply.

You tell yourself you're fine. You're above it. But then you replay the conversations, dissect the timing, reread the texts.

You're not needy. You're human.

And rejection hurts more when you were honest. When you showed your real self. When you let someone in. It's not weakness - it's evidence you were *brave*.

We say we want real, but when real shows up, not everyone can handle it.

The Self-Worth Reset

Here's the truth: someone rejecting you doesn't downgrade your value. It just narrows your audience.

Not everyone has the capacity to receive you. Not everyone deserves to.

You've been told you're too much. Loud. Extra. Difficult to love. And maybe you are…
I may not be your cup of tea, but I'm someone's triple-shot vodka with a lime wedge and no regrets.

Your worth isn't dependent on being chosen. Your worth is steady, unbothered, unchanging - even when they ghost. Even when they scroll past. Even when they don't call back.

You are not a product. You are a person. And you're not here for mass appeal; you're here for real connection.

You're not a discount version of yourself just because someone didn't pick you.

The Petty Phase (and Why It's Necessary)

You *will* stalk their socials.
You *will* screenshot the chat.
You *might* send one last text you'll pretend you regret.

You'll rage-vent. You'll get dramatic. You'll tell your friends the same story five times.

It's okay. There's nothing radical about bypassing your pain in the name of self-respect. Feel it. Wallow in it if you must. Just don't unpack and live there.

Your pettiness is the bridge between being devastated and being over it. Let it do its job.

Light a candle. Block them. Cry while wearing heavy eyeliner.

The Unexpected Glow-Up

Rejection sharpens you. Rage clears the space.

You start walking differently. Dressing louder. Laughing bigger. You start making decisions that are for you - not for their reaction.

You become magnetic. Not because you're trying. Because you've stopped performing.

You take better care of yourself, not out of spite, but reverence. You upgrade your routine. You delete the playlist. You unfollow the ex.

They don't come back because you changed. They come back because you did what they never thought you would: move on without them.

The Mirror Test

Look at yourself.

Not filtered. Not face-tuned. Just you. In your power. In your pain. In your evolution.

The person who was once broken, now standing. The version of you they didn't get to keep. The Empress in recovery.

You're not waiting to be validated. You're busy being *undeniable*.

And the mirror? It doesn't lie. It reflects strength. It reflects softness. It reflects someone who has stopped asking for emotional leftovers.

Radical Self-Worth

Radical self-worth isn't just affirmations and bath bombs. It's saying:

"I still love myself - even when they didn't."
"I know my value - even when they couldn't see it."
"I choose me - even when it hurts."

It's keeping your standards high - even when you're lonely. It's not begging. It's deleting the thread. It's rewriting the story.

It's staying single longer than you expected, because you'd rather wait for the one who *sees* you than settle for the one who *missed* you.

It's forgiving yourself for wanting someone who wasn't worthy.

It's trusting that one day, someone will meet you where you are - and you won't have to shrink to fit.

Because you are not disposable. You are not an almost. You are not a phase. You are permanent. And the Empress always returns to herself.

Next chapter: The Power of Being Underestimated.

Chapter 11: The Power of Being Underestimated

Let them think you're soft. Let them think you're sweet. Let them think you're not a threat. And then rise.

There's a strange power in being underestimated. In being dismissed, overlooked, or quietly condescended to. Because while they're sleeping on you, you're strategising. While they're downplaying you, you're developing. While they're talking, you're becoming.

Let's talk about turning doubt into dominance. And why being underestimated is the most underrated advantage.

The Dismissal Diaries

You've heard it before:

"She's nice, but…"
"She's a bit much."
"I just don't see her as leadership."

Translation? You scared them.

They've smiled while secretly betting against you. They've called you "Queen" and then stolen your ideas. They've confused your kindness for compliance. Or worse, your composure for consent. Darling, you're so fake. China denied making you.

You remember every one of them. Not because they hurt you, but because they helped you sharpen. You've got a mental Excel sheet titled 'Watch This Space' and their names are all colour coded.

The Weapon of Surprise

There is nothing more powerful than the woman they didn't see coming.

The one they thought would cry who kept calm. The one they thought would fold who held the line. The one they thought was ornamental who turned out to be *operational*.

They underestimated you because you wore glam makeup during the day and a high pony. Because you asked questions. Because you didn't speak in corporate PowerPoint tone.

You let them make the mistake. And then you made the move.

The Sweetness Strategy

Your softness is not a weakness. It's camouflage.

You can hold space *and* hold boundaries. You can speak gently *and* carry fire. You can nod politely while internally filing every red flag for later removal.

They don't see you coming because they expect rage to be loud. They forget that some assassins wear Chanel.

Don't downplay your kindness. Just don't weaponise it against yourself either.

You're not here to be palatable. You're here to be powerful, with a nice blow wave and a vengeance playlist.

The Power in the Quiet

You don't always have to announce your next move. Sometimes power is found in the pause.

Let them think you're resting.
Let them think you're confused.
Let them think you're cute.

Meanwhile, you're building something. Planning something. Becoming someone, they'll wish they'd paid attention to sooner.

You don't owe them visibility.

You owe yourself progress.

Restraint isn't weakness. It's strategy. It's giving them enough rope to do what they always do, while you quietly buy the company.

Watch Me Energy

You used to defend yourself. Now you just deliver.

You stopped explaining your potential and started demonstrating it. You let the results speak. And when the time comes, you make your entrance, not with noise, but with undeniable presence.

"Watch me" isn't always a roar. Sometimes it's a whisper that hits like thunder.

You don't have to clap back. You clap forward, with every step, every success, every "actually, I'll pass."

The Empress in Disguise

They saw you as quiet. You were calculating.
They saw you as average. You were evolving.
They saw you as temporary. You were inevitable.

You weren't invisible. You were observant. You were learning. Taking notes. Highlighting behaviour in neon yellow.

Being underestimated gave you a front-row seat to who people *really* are when they think they've already won.

And you? You stayed seated, stayed silent, and stayed scheming.

Because the Empress doesn't rush. She rises.

The Petty Advantage

Yes, you remembered what they said.
Yes, you saw them roll their eyes in that meeting.
Yes, you clocked that one friend who said, "You can't say that."

You're not bitter. You're organised.

You don't need revenge. You just need to keep going and maybe smile when they ask how you
got there.

And when you do succeed? Be gracious. But let them know the crown is custom fitted.

Why It Works

Because the world doesn't expect women to rise quietly. They expect tantrums. They expect tears. They expect you to fall apart publicly.

But you didn't. You put on your best coat, you fixed your lip liner, and you kept it moving.

Your power wasn't just in proving them wrong. It was in not

needing their belief to begin with.

Laugh While You Climb

Because sometimes the best revenge is not success, it's laughing so hard your wrinkle freeze cracks.

You laugh at the guy who said you were "too intense." You laugh at the manager who thought you'd never leave.
You laugh at the mirror, because damn, you really did that.

And not for them. For you.

The underestimated woman becomes the most unstoppable. Because while they were watching someone else, you built a throne.

And now they're asking if you're hiring.

Next chapter: Men, Money, and the Myth of Being Chosen.

Chapter 12: Men, Money, and the Myth of Being Chosen

You are not the prize. You are the selector. And your life is not an audition for someone else's approval.

We were raised on Cinderella stories and songs about being picked. As if being chosen is the highest honour a woman can earn. Be pretty. Be nice. Be agreeable. Be the one he chooses.

Cinderella waited for a man with footwear. We ordered ours online, on sale and walked out.

Let's talk about the myth of being chosen, and the power of

choosing yourself first, last, and always.

The Pageant Conditioning

It starts early. Be good. Be polite. Be pleasing. You're told not to take up too much space.
Not to talk too loudly. Don't be too smart, too sexy, too serious. Just enough to be... what? Acceptable? Pickable?

The unspoken message: your worth is tied to your desirability. To being picked.

As if a man looking at you and thinking "she'll do" is some kind of award.

The Audition Phase

You've done it.

Pretended to love football.

Laughed at jokes that weren't funny.
Changed your outfit because he didn't like the bold colour.

You've bent, softened, and shape shifted. Not out of love, but out of hope. Hope that if you're perfect enough, accommodating enough, he'll finally pick you. Claim you. Stay.

You weren't dating. You were auditioning.

The Financial Fantasy

They used to say, "Marry rich." Now it's "Split everything 50/50" but he still expects to use all of yours, a clean house, shaved legs, and emotional labour with a smile.

Here's the plot twist: your independence doesn't mean you owe anyone access.

Money doesn't buy power. Alignment does.
You don't want a wallet. You want a partner.

You're Not Being Chosen - You're Choosing

What if you're the table? The house? The land?
You're not the picked flower. You're the whole beautiful garden.

You are not an application. You are an invitation.
You don't need to shrink yourself for someone to feel tall next to you. You don't need to impress him with your cooking skills and yoga butt.

You're not on trial. You're the jury.

The Delusion Detox

You had the Pinterest board ready. The Instagram captions drafted. His last name sounded okay with yours. And then… nothing.

He ghosted. Or breadcrumbed. Or called you "intense" because you asked what the hell was going on.

And there it was: the myth cracked.

Being picked doesn't mean anything if it comes from someone who can't even hold a conversation without correcting you or cutting you off.

You deserve more than a maybe. You deserve someone who shows up fully. Or nothing at all.

High Standards Are Not Arrogance

Wanting emotional intelligence, ambition, generosity, and monogamy is not high maintenance.

It's high value.

You're not asking for a superhero. You're asking for a grown adult with empathy and a decent pair of sheets.

If he thinks that's too much - he's not enough.

The Choice Is Yours

You choose how you're treated. You choose who gets access. You choose your boundaries, your pace, your peace.

And when the old voice whispers, "But what if I end up alone?" - you remind her:

Alone isn't scary. Settling is.

Because the real glow-up isn't a ring. It's a life you built without disrespect and begging for the bare minimum.

Next chapter: Age, Appearance, and Other People's Projections.

Chapter 13: Age, Appearance, and Other People's Projections

Your body is not an apology. Your age is not a crisis. And your shine has nothing to do with Botox.

Let's talk about getting older, about the unsolicited opinions, the beauty myths, the internal tug-of-war between self-acceptance and society's "before and after" nonsense.

You are not a relic. You're a revelation.

The Birthday Breakdown

Thirty was cute, but forty came in fast. Suddenly, everyone wants to talk about skincare, fillers, and "anti-aging," like time is a disease.

You go to a party and someone says, "You look good - for your age." For your age?

Like it's a condition. Like youth is the currency, and you're bankrupt.

You don't need to look young. You need to look *like you*.

The Hair Panic

It starts with one grey hair. A glint of silver near your temple. You freeze.

Is this it?

You Google. You pluck. You panic.

Then you realise: nobody died. You didn't lose your spark. Your hair didn't send a text to your ex.

It's just hair. And it's kind of badass.

You're not falling apart. You're unfolding.

The Body Rebrand

The jeans fit differently. The arms wave longer than your hand. You catch your reflection and think, "Was that there yesterday?"

Your body has lived. It's stored joy, heartbreak, carbs, cortisol, trauma, tequila, and time.

And guess what? It's still carrying you.

You don't need to bounce back. You need to move forward with grace, strength, and a killer bra.

The Projection Trap

Everyone has opinions about how you should look:

Too done. Too undone.

Too thin. Too thick.
Too much makeup. Too natural.
Try harder. Age gracefully.
Just try not to look like you're trying.
You could be in a sequin jumpsuit standing under a disco ball, and they'd still say, "Didn't you wear that last week?"

They'll say you let yourself go if you stop dyeing your hair.
They'll say you're trying too hard if you start wearing lashes.

You'll never win the game because it was never designed for you to. So, get out of it.

The Mirror Reclaim

You used to check for flaws. Now you check for *truth*.

Is this who I am? Yes.

Is this who I'm becoming? Even better.

Your reflection isn't a warning sign. It's a love letter.

You don't need to look younger. You need to look proud.

Real Is the New Beautiful

The laugh lines are from laughing. The stretch marks are from living. The softness is from surviving.

Let people say what they want.

You're not living for their gaze; you're living for your own grace.

Because beauty isn't perfection. Its presence.

You walked through fire. And you still showed up.

That's the most stunning thing about you.

Next chapter: Forgiveness, Forgetting, and the Final Block.

Chapter 14: Forgiveness, Forgetting, and the Final Block

Forgiveness is freedom. But blocking is peace. And sometimes the real healing comes with a side of "goodbye."

We've been told to forgive. To let go. To take the high road. And sure, forgiveness can be powerful. But so can boundaries. So can walking away without offering a final monologue or a coffee.

Let's talk about healing - not the polite kind, the real kind.

Forgiveness Without Access

You can forgive someone, and still never want to see them again.
You can forgive and still block.
You can forgive and still unfollow, delete, mute, and never speak their name again.

Forgiveness is for *you*. Not them.

It doesn't mean what they did was okay.
It means *you're* okay enough to stop rehearsing the pain.

The Myth of Closure

Closure's marketed like a gift. It's usually self-assembled.

You wait for an apology.
You wait for the truth.
You wait for one last conversation that explains it all.

Sometimes you get it. Sometimes you don't.

But the truth? Closure is a decision, not a discussion.

It's the moment you say: I'm done needing clarity from chaos.

The Ghost File

They disappeared.
No explanation. No goodbye. Just... Silence of the Lambs.

You didn't deserve it. You didn't cause it. But now you're left holding a story with no ending.

So, here's what you do:

You stop rereading the last message.
You stop checking if they're online.
You stop letting their absence define your narrative.

You write your own ending: "Blocked, blessed, and back to life."

The Apology You'll Never Get

They won't say sorry.

Not because you don't deserve it, but because they don't have the capacity to offer it.

They'll rewrite the story. Minimise it. Forget it. You don't have to.

You don't need their words to validate your pain. You already lived it. That's enough.

When Forgiveness Feels Fake

Sometimes you're not ready. Sometimes it feels forced. Sometimes forgiveness feels like a betrayal *of yourself*.

It's okay.

You don't have to rush your healing for the comfort of others. You don't owe anyone grace they haven't earned.

Forgiveness isn't one big holy act. It's a slow burn.

The Final Block

There's something sacred about blocking.
It's not petty. It's not dramatic. It's not immature.

It's a digital boundary with real-world impact.

You're not punishing them. You're protecting yourself.

Your new standard is simple:

If it costs your peace, it's too expensive.
If someone makes you feel guilty for protecting your energy, access denied.
Boundaries aren't about locking people out.
They're about inviting the right people in and knowing you don't have to throw a parade every time someone knocks.

You are not an all-access pass. You are the event.
And entry is by invitation only, no walk-ins, no plus-ones, and absolutely no man-babies in greasy man buns.
You're not being cruel. You're being clear.
You're not hiding. You're choosing peace over surveillance.

Sometimes healing means deleting the entire thread.

The Clean Break Club

You leave. You stop explaining. You let people misunderstand.

You stop re-engaging just because it's polite. You stop being available just because they're sorry *now*.

You've graduated. And you're not obligated to stay in rooms or situations you've outgrown.

Healing Without a Witness

No one needs to know how hard it was. No one needs to see the struggle.

Sometimes the most profound healing happens in quiet.

No announcement. No reveal. Just a better you who no longer bleeds from the same wound.

You forgave. Or maybe you didn't. But you moved on.

And that's more than enough.

Next chapter: The Empress Era.

Chapter 15: The Empress Era

This is not your comeback. This is your arrival.

You've cried, burned out, been ghosted, underestimated, rejected, stretched thin, laughed at, and written off.

And yet - here you are.

Let's talk about the era where you stop surviving and start *reigning*.

No More Shrinking

You don't squeeze yourself into spaces anymore. You don't make yourself digestible.

You don't say "just kidding" after every opinion.

You speak.
You stay.
You shine.

And if someone thinks you're too much? They can go find less.

You Are the Standard

You don't ask for permission.

You don't water yourself down for room temperature people.

You walk in like you own the floor - and suddenly, everyone believes you do.

You are the blueprint. The energy shift. The new normal.

Audacity Activated

You wear what you want. You say what needs to be said. You rest when you need to.

You post the picture. You say no. You don't chase. You raise your rate. You raise your standard. You raise your eyebrow.

You are no longer available for things that dull you.

You're not an open bar anymore. You're a private lounge. And access is earned, not assumed or paid for.

Celebration Without Comparison

You no longer need to be the best. You just need to be *yours*.

You stop comparing timelines, bank accounts, thighs, and relationships.

You stop measuring your life against someone's curated content.

Because you realised: you're not late. You're not behind. You're *right on time*.

Softness as Strength

You love without fear. You rest without guilt.

You feel everything and still move forward.

That is strength.
That is Empress energy.

It's not about being hard. It's about being *whole*.

Rewriting the Rules

You don't want a throne. You want freedom.

You don't need to be admired. You want to be understood.

You don't need to prove anything. You just *are*.

You rewrite the story. You take your power back. You hold your head high and your boundaries higher.

And when they ask what changed? Everything.

Because you did.

The Empress Manifesto

I do not apologise for my power.

I do not wait to be chosen.

I do not keep peace that costs my dignity.

I do not shrink.

I do not chase.

I do not explain myself to people committed to misunderstanding me.

I walk in my truth.

I speak with fire.

I love without shame.

This is my era.

Not a phase.

Not a chapter.

A reign.

Long live the Empress.

Empress Restored

www.ingramcontent.com/pod-product-compliance
Lightning Source LLC
Chambersburg PA
CBHW061731070526
44583CB00024B/3095